What Hummingbirds Do

poems by

Louise Cary Barden

Finishing Line Press
Georgetown, Kentucky

What Hummingbirds Do

ACKNOWLEDGMENTS

Thanks to the keen eye and good instincts of my friend and fellow poet, Rachel
Barton, for her help in assembling this collection.

Thanks to my fellow poets in 3Rivers Poetry—Frank Babcock, Brigitte Goetz, Karen
Jones, and Doug Stone —for their helpful comments on drafts of many of these
poems. And thanks to my companions in Live Poets for their valuable ideas and
response during the writing process.

Especially, thanks to the editors of the journals where these poems first appeared:

Calyx, 2018 Lois Cranston Memorial Prize—What Hummingbirds Do
Cathexis Northwest—We ponder the destiny of our country and our lives
Circle of Seasons—Saving the Garden
Gleam: Journal of the Cadralor—Viewpoint
humana obscura—Under a Changing Sky
Kosmos—Butterfly Effect
Sow's Ear—Looking for Jeffers' House, Potter's Shop
Timberline Review—Reflections at the Checkout
Verseweavers (Oregon Poetry Association)—Ghazal in June
Willawaw Journal—To my Great-Grandmother, Into the World, October Song, On
Drifts, Our Second Year, Taking Stock, In the Moonlight

Publisher: Leah Huete de Maines
Editor: Christen Kincaid
Cover Art: Louise Cary Barden and Donna Meinhold
Author Photo: Larry Barden
Cover Design: Elizabeth Maines McCleavy

Order online: www.finishinglinepress.com
also available on amazon.com

Author inquiries and mail orders:
Finishing Line Press
PO Box 1626
Georgetown, Kentucky 40324
USA

Contents

To Larry
with love and thanks
for his decades of encouragement
while enduring life with a poet
and to
Jeff and Teresa
Thaddeus and Juniper

for Jeff
To my Great-Grandmother
In case the post office is still delivering where you are

Granny, I sit in the garden reading the letter you wrote
your sister when you were the same age I am now.

Lena, I guess I'll never get to see the orange trees in Florida. I'm too old
to travel and my eyes don't work as well as they used to.

Now I know how you felt. But unlike you, I made it—lots of times, in fact.
    If I could
I'd send you pictures of the groves, verdant branches hung with
    glowing fruit,

and pictures of my mother, your granddaughter, living there. After
    she died,
I found a postcard you sent me, its one-cent stamp postmarked

at the Memphis train station on your way home. Your familiar
    cramped cursive
has faded with age: *Cry loud if they aren't treating you all right.*
    I'll come get you.

Here in my backyard, ruddy penstemons crowd purple salvia spikes
and flannel milkweed. Bees hum a song of autumn coming soon
    among the asters

and the daisies' last summer snow. My dahlias explode red as your
    strawberry jam,
those jars you filled with sweetness and lined up on pantry shelves
    in pre-dawn light

before your daughter woke and fussed about you messing up
    her kitchen once again.
That morning you led me out the back door at sunrise. There was
    something

I should see. We walked together past Grandmother's neat beds of
    hybrid roses
to the far back lot, to where a wire fence embraced your tangle of
    stems, leaves,

flowers whose names I no longer know. Granny, once when
        someone asked me
the time and place I felt the safest and most loved, I remembered

holding your hand beside your garden, crowded as this one I sit
        beside today.
You pointed to a web where day's first light split gold through hanging dew,

and at the center a fragile ladder spun by the great black-and-yellow spider
suspended there. You said, *Look. Look how beautiful it is.*

On the Edge of Sunrise

What the young do not know—ghosts
      follow us
      into the day, sunlight breaking around those wisps,
      those forms touching
      but not touching the ground.
      Reach out.
      The untouchable
      just beyond your fingertips stands and calls.
        (We believe you, Hamlet. He is here.)

      Vapor. The past, almost visible.
      There.   It speaks!
         (whisper)

The young cannot hear. They do not listen.
      We who are old   stand frozen,
                    struck   dumb,
      air filled with the weight of words,
      invisible letters growing… into a heap around us.
        (What is worth keeping?)

      What shall we do with all that history? We
      teeter on infinity, unable
      to halt
      the wall, the past. Stories grow.   Books.
      Immovable pile around us.
        (phantoms murmuring)

      We cannot lift   the letters,   pass   words
      on to hands, arms   strong enough
      to carry them
      to the living.

Sun rises. Shades
      move on (whisper… shhhh).
      We hear.   All those words—
      we stand trapped inside the great cone, the past.
      (history never came easily).
Haze   dissolves into day's glare.
      The shapes beckon

Viewpoint

1.
Breeze riffles the still water, pushes
white waterlilies tight against each other
like boats rafting together for a holiday.
Turtle hatchlings lift their heads above
the surface, like thin bubbles breaking.

2.
By the red backdoor, a crate holds empty
bottles and a scribbled note requesting butter
with the day's delivered milk. There was
so much we expected. We did not know
we had so much that we could one day lose.

3.
July birches lean out as if to see their own
green whispers reflected in a mirror
or the glow of their October gold and yellow
shouts. In January snow, silent trunks reach,
white and black, for something in the sky.

4.
The attic ceiling slopes almost to the floor, too
low, even at its center peak, for an adult to stand
at the top of the stairs. It guards the toy room
against inquisitive parents—a child-sized
folding table, tumbled dolls, a miniature train.

5.
I am three, on a shady hill above a pond.
It is a new place. My father holds my hand.
Trees around us rustle in the soft wind
and a dog barks, at a house down the road.
I can see my whole life in front of me.

Into the World

Nine. And-a-half. I stand
under the white pine behind our house.
Check around. No one
watching. Grab the bottom branch
sticky with pitch, pull up.
Anchor one sneakered foot on top of the limb
against the scarred trunk,
draw the other up to stand firm,
and reach
to keep going. Who can tell how far?
Still time. Mama's inside
cooking supper. Still time
before I have to stand
with my sister at the soapy sink of dishes
washing and drying
while we fight. I'm up
branch after branch. Past
sagging gutters
full of leaves and the bottom edge
of black shingles. Up into sap-
scented air, needles' soft prickle
in my palms. Up.
Past the highest point I've ever been,
moving even after
my sister suddenly yells, "Stop!"
far below. Tattletail sister. I
barely slow when the tapered trunk
narrows, begins
to sway,
taking my frail frame
with it. Too late for anyone
to make me quit now. I climb
until at last I can see over the shingled ridge
the front yard marigolds, the line
of my friends' rooftops
along our narrow street
all the way to an unbroken
dome of cottony sky.

Sister still yells and I stand on a branch
so thin it bends
under my feet. I ride
the wind. I hang on
long enough to get a good look—
new treetops, chimneys, the shiny
tops of cars on the big road
outside our neighborhood.
Long enough to glimpse
the whole world, all
the places I haven't been yet,
until Mama's clear voice
pierces the haze of green I've come through,
until her threat brings me down.

October Song

In the trees a mad flurry of warblers—
Cape May, Tennessee, Black-and White, Chestnut-Sided—
spring colors gone drab for winter. Their beaks
work the last leaves. No singing now.

Cape May, Tennessee, Black-and White, Chestnut-Sided
dart here and there through gray branches
to work the last leaves. No singing now.
They come zigzagging down,

dart here and there through gray branches
like snowflakes already covering peaks in Wyoming.
They come zigzagging down,
whirling wings and brown feathers over the ground

like snowflakes already covering peaks in Wyoming.
I want to fly north where the world glitters white,
whirl wings and brown feathers over the ground
to hear fresh Arctic wind singing now.

I want to fly north where the world glitters white,
away from spring colors gone drab for winter,
to hear fresh Arctic wind singing now
in the trees like a flurry of warblers.

Butterfly Effect

Next September, find a view above an Appalachian
gap—the place where a ridge of rolling mountain tops
declines into a break, hillsides dipping and rising
on either side of a narrow trail made by paws and moccasins
and boots. Stand in the cold before sunrise where,
in the shadow of those hills, the leafy tops of oak
and poplar, ash and walnut seem feathered gray
and beige in misty air below. And wait.

Wait for the sun's first gold to strike that canopy, transform
the mist into a thin vapor and warm the pale feathers
into orange opening wings, a hundred then a thousand
glowing spots fanning out into an auburn blanket
over every branch above the dew-soaked slopes' dark
green rhododendron tangles. Stand sun-struck
as those new-lit wings begin to rise in twos and threes, more
and more bright sparks flickering into the blue
until they become silhouettes and gather
into a cloud that vanishes off into southern sky.

If a billion fewer Monarchs traverse the air's
invisible road today than twenty years ago, what difference
can it make? Scientists say the flutter of just one butterfly's wings
can change the weather days from now. They do not know
a way to calculate what that change will be
among the million possibilities; they call their study
chaos theory. While volcanic ash covers farms in the Pacific
and firestorms roar across the Australian Bush, those mathematicians
leave us here without a cause that can be named
to stand high on this ridge, transfixed by glowing flames
as they ascend into the sun.

If a Tree Falls

It was enough that our parents pulled us like carrots
from the tight busy little neighborhood we had always loved,
the cramped bungalow by a pond,
surrounded by more cramped bungalows all filled
with kids we had always known. They pulled us
away from the woods at the end of our rough
little street, uprooted us from our solid ground
of stick forts and hideouts in the trees, swimming holes
and warm winter playrooms with low ceilings
tucked under the eaves of tiny houses.

They spread our family out in separate bedrooms
in a windy Victorian farmhouse on the edge of a cornfield,
without another house or kid in sight. Then they put
my closest sister and me onto a bus that bounced,
and stopped, and started up forever to a strange
elementary school, to classrooms where the teachers
didn't know we were the students who always
raised our hands and always added to the row of stars
beside our names on the reading chart.

That day, I sat I friendless at the desk I'd been assigned
while my new teacher, who had already shown
she didn't like my essays, droned on about a tree
that fell in a wild forest, where there were no kids
or houses. She talked and talked about a falling tree
no one would ever make into a fort, and she asked,
"Was there a sound if no one was there to hear?"

She asked as if we, sitting at our little desks with inkwells
and heavy lift-up tops on black hinges, should know
the answer. She waited while hands shot up
all around. Then she looked straight at me
and asked again, "Was there a sound?" as if
I might think it mattered.

On Drifts

The whole day before Palm Sunday we watched
snow blow sideways against the windows
of our Massachusetts farmhouse,
needles so sharp they pierced
your cheeks if you went out
bundled to the ears and wool capped.
Then dawn, dazzling under clear sky.
Eight feet of cold powder
covered the quarter-mile to the street
where Dad had parked our car before the storm.
Church stood another seven miles away.

Sitting now in a counselor's office,
childhood and religion left behind for thirty years,
I keep remembering the way we four girls
left our flowered Easter dresses in the closet,
pulled on wool pants under skirts,
laced up boots, zipped heavy jackets
and floundered out to make a path into the drifts.
Shovels failed. One last freeze before sunrise
had hardened a crust too thick to dig,
too thin to walk on, and left the apple orchard's
black branches painted with it, shining.

Which one of us discovered how
to get from house to car I can't recall.
The secret was to use the principle of physics
that makes things float, the first lesson in swimming
when we learned to put our faces down, reach out arms and legs.
That Palm Sunday when we sank chest deep in cold,
we floundered up again to spread ourselves
across the unmarked frozen surface.
We almost swam our way to church
with clumsy, careful breast strokes we had taught ourselves.

How To Cross Prairie Portage

Beach your canoe on the rocks.
Carry it down a spruce trail

To the bay. Take your place in the line leading
To a weathered cabin under

The Canadian flag. Camp guides,
A long-limbed college girl

And blonde boy, who hold plastic bags
Of border-crossing permits, flirt

While their charges lounge on rocks
By the water. Fishermen

Plot a route to the biggest
Northern Pike. Rain falls lightly

And warm. An hour passes. Two.
The campers spread peanut butter

On squashed bread. Something small
And furry scurries across the trail.

A Canadian Ranger calls *Next*.
Show papers with checked boxes and

Official signatures, your little gas stove,
A map. Free to go.

Scrape of canoe on gravel. Ahead a glint of light
On waves, dark forests. A loon laughs,

Eagle circles above. Paddles move.
The start of something.

Our Second Year

After April rains, when the Mulberry rose over its rock islands,
rushed above willows on the shore,
we borrowed a canoe,
ready for roar after roar of water, sudden
angles of current.

We hauled onto banks above falls,
and walked ahead to plot
our course—hard left, sharp
right, straight down the chute, careening
on, sweeping paddles in rhythm, muscles strained.
Tips of willows bent
as we streamed by, honeysuckle
tangles and beds of lady slippers
disappearing in woods on either side.

A stony hazard finally threw us, wild
catapult to frigid water. No life
jackets, just the will
to surface in a stretch of slow stream.
We laughed as we stroked for our drifting craft.
A little fire to dry our clothes, a cup of hot coffee.
Thirty sets of rapids

before we slept
in our double sleeping bag.
We didn't dream of August, the coming
time without rain. On our cloud-swollen river,
we didn't see ourselves sitting
apart, too hot to touch, while tomatoes
shriveled and marigolds turned brown.
In the spring rush we couldn't imagine
the life without water.

The Dazzling Invisibility

We sit at a picnic table by the Arkansas River
talking with my husband's friends, as overhead
a thousand white wings appear against the blue
to spiral and rise all together, fold their circle
back on itself, rise again until I stand head back
watching black-tipped feathers
shimmer and tilt, grey
and glow in the sun.

I pull my husband's arm and point. He turns
to look up at the shifting stream of birds,
the way it wheels and whirls, tips
and glints against the light. He whispers to me
long enough to say it happens every fall,
these ibis gliding south above the water,
and turns back to conversation.

The next day in a downtown parking lot
he chats with an old friend about what's changed
as we walk to see the new-built library and
the shopping plaza going up nearby. I
fall behind, then stop, frozen, gazing

into a sky that's split by patterned coils of moving wings,
the gleam of silver, white and black
as feathers flash and sparkle,
gather into waves that circle, glide
until they shrink to dots along the far horizon,
disappear.

The footsteps and the voices fade away. I'm
left alone to watch
the shining cloud
the others have seen so many times
they think they know it well.

Revelation: Patmos

*"I ...heard behind me a great voice, as of a trumpet, saying, I am
Alpha and Omega, the first and the last...."*
John, The Revelator: Revelation 22

Let's say the tourist is standing
on the hillside stairs, the cruise ship
and all the Mediterranean
spread out below her, a hundred
tiled rooftops almost at her feet. She
has already been guided through
the monastery behind her, urged to wonder
at two-thousand years of manuscripts
painstakingly rendered and unstintingly
embellished with gold,
the torturous depictions
of Christ stretched on the Cross,
the ornate calligraphy perfect in every line.

She has already stood in the cave
behind a rope separating her from the grotto,
the source of God's voice—the space
so bedecked in paintings, so covered by centuries
of monks' art and icons
the split rock was scarcely visible. Even
the stone entrance itself
hid inside white stucco walls,
behind a heavy wooden door.
Perhaps she thinks, *So little left
to really see.*

But still, on the steps, John
stands behind her, his gaunt frame
almost touching her left shoulder.
Without looking she knows
he is dirty, covered in dust,
with the smell of a man
who lives in a cave on a dry island. She
sees him there alone
month after month after year,
under the low rock ceiling, before
the sudden boom. The earthquake
and the split…
The Voice….

then from far below,
the ship's great horn, the calling.

Ghazal in June

In summer heat your body wants to feel the wind
until you wish that you could steal the wind.

The world's a fragrant orange, sweet and juicy ripe,
the scent you catch under its tender peel, the wind.

This hour has brought green leaf and purple flower
and to the feathered spread of blue-winged teal the wind.

Clouds, trees, the chirp and churk of birds fade fast
leaving behind one thing that's real, the wind.

Do not think of snow blown cold for months ahead
when each new winter storm carries in its creel the wind.

The sails are raised, your wooden tiller set on course.
What guides your boat upon its keel? The wind.

You turn to leave so fast he cannot say goodbye
while sun is in his eyes and at your heel the wind.

One Last Day to Paddle

Along the river's edge, trees still green but tinged gold,
gilded as if with summer's wealth just before the end. Purple asters
drag to ground with their own weight, dahlias explode
into great clouds, red and yellow, as if they can't
put out enough petals to stop the march of winter

coming on, the end of green, the last of the roses' red
fragrance. In other places I have called my home
near the Atlantic, these were the days of sudden frost, trees
dipped overnight in burgundy and copper, days
that warned of cold ahead as sharp as pre-election speeches.

I've never been a fan of fall, that erratic harbinger of death
that is not death. This year summer slides away into Pacific
fog. Clouds that do not lift melt to weeks of rain. Daylight
shortens to the smallest nub as politicians heat the air with words.
Mink in winter coats hop from rock to rock along the shore.

Two sides. The same nickel
for Betsy

Every night my sister stood beside me at the kitchen sink.
While one of us submerged her pudgy hands in foam
and water growing cold around the dishes and the dinner glasses as
      they clinked
against the porcelain bowl, the other took each tumbler as if it were a loan

from pudgy hands that had been submerged in foam
to rinse and dry and pile it on a growing stack.
Out of the porcelain bowl, each tumbler felt as if it were a loan
we knew we could not drop or crack

but had to rinse and dry and pile it on a growing stack
at ages eight and ten, as if it were a game we had to play
although we knew we could not drop or crack
a single one. We knew we were required to stay

at ages eight and ten, as if it were a game we had to play
until the after-dinner chore was done. We could not leave
a single one. We knew we were required to stay
while Mama put the babies—two or three or four—to sleep.

Until the after-dinner chore was done we could not leave.
As we grew older, every night one washed and the other dried
while Mama put the younger kids—two or three or four—to sleep.
I waited, quiet, for the time when I could leave; my sister
      sometimes yelled or cried.

As we grew older, every night one washed and the other dried
until at last I went to find a life out on my own.
I had waited, quiet, for the time when I could leave; my sister
      sometimes yelled or cried
two more years until she too could say she'd grown.

After I went to find a life out on my own
our separate lives curved off and far away. We rarely felt the need
      to keep in touch
those two years until she too could say she'd grown
and she went to college, love and marriage. We didn't call each other much.

Our separate lives curved off and far away. We rarely felt the need to
    keep in touch.
We spent our days and hours just as we wished, apart.
She went to college, love and marriage. We didn't call each other much.
We had babies. We got jobs. We each thought it was a start.

We spent our days and hours as we wished, apart,
except now and then for just a little talk.
We had babies. We got jobs. We each saw it as a start.
We'd visit with our men and kids, and we two would take a walk.

Now and then we needed just a little talk,
about our siblings and our kids, her teaching and my marketing
    career. We'd ask advice.
We planned more visits with our men, and we two would take a walk.
We told each other all the ways we'd learned life's prizes can
    exact a price.

We talked about our siblings and our kids (now grown), our jobs,
    and we gave advice.
We watched our father's death, saw Mom's need for company and care.
We told each other all the ways we'd learned life's prizes always had a price.
While our younger siblings built careers, we saw we had to share

the space left by our father's death, Mom's need for company and care
as she grew old. We took her to the doctor and to church. We helped
    her shop
while our younger siblings built careers. We shared
her hours at doctors and in hospitals and went with her to Sunday school.
    Before it stopped.

As Mom grew old we took her to the doctor and to church. We helped
    her shop.
We split the time we knew she needed help. Good girls, we traded
hours with her at doctors and hospitals and went with her to Sunday school.
    Before it stopped.
I stood alone—Mom alive, still needing care. My sister dead.

We split the time we knew our mother needed help. Good girls, we traded
hours that grew cold as water around dishes and the fragile glasses we
    once clinked
until I stood alone—Mom alive, still needing care. My sister dead.
And me with just those nights she stood beside me at the kitchen sink.

We ponder the destiny of our country and our lives
The week before Election Day, 2020

Cassandra can cry out all she wants,
but this can't be stopped any more than water
can stop itself from dropping over the cliff.
See what happens? Without earth under the water
there is nothing to hold the stream together—nothing
to make the water remember the way its molecules
moved all as one under a clear sky. Suddenly
without the riverbed to hold the river
up, every drop flies unfettered, wild,
shattering against the jagged stones below
split into droplets transformed to fleeting vapor.

See how they rise invisibly?
Each small molecule set free, ascending
until the day they meet to form in a cloud, gathering
into drops again, uniting again to fall and stream again. Is this
how everything must work—this joining and parting, this falling
from rock ledges, this splintering far below the heights
against the tumbled stones of lost mountainsides? The drops
that once were joined—set free? Or are they driven out
to gleam and perish on their own?
Is this how we must pass the days
and decades growing into eons—as matter
forming and exploding, nations rising to dominion
and then failing? Is this our foretold union—each molecule
and droplet ordained to bind with others?
Each union breaking into pieces, without will
or foreknowledge? Each of us alone and moving forward
as if we know where we're going?

Right around the corner

Suddenly here he is,
just when I stopped
preparing myself. Here,
where I least
expected it, the old familiar
figure in black leans
casually against a building, tip
of the scythe
resting on the brick wall, deep eyes
fixed blank on the horizon.

No hurry, just
waiting. Not even
noticing afternoon commuters
as they scurry down the sidewalk to their cars,
their homes. As if
he has nothing to do
with them, nothing
to do at all now that my mother and sister
are dead.
The old liar.
He turns his head, stares straight
into my face, as if I am already late
for our appointment.

He watches without a word, without
a sign. What can I do
but walk fast,
fast. What price will he exact
unless I move ahead, heels
clicking on the concrete—walk
as if the sister I still have
isn't waiting for her biopsy results,

walk as if I already know
my scan two days ago
has come back negative, walk
as if I am breathing, as if this time
he has nothing,
not a single thing
to do with me.

Under A Changing Sky
for Teresa

All winter, those dreary weeks at home,
it seems no ray of sun can be allowed
through endless days ceilinged with low clouds.
Rain's constant throb goes on against the ground
until the summer's last baked clay has drowned
in slippery mud and rain-soaked leaves that crowd
against black flowers autumn frost has bowed
on stems bent into what seems a frown.

And yet on days dark enough to cause despair,
a sudden break above, a shaft of light
spills across the dreary sleeping land
and turns it gold, as the once grey air
glows incandescent, rainbow hues so bright
they could be the reflection of a greater hand.

Reflections at the Checkout

I keep forgetting I'm a woman
who wears diamonds.
Diamonds, with an S, not just
one well-bred solitaire. Diamonds,
bound into a platinum pool
on my right hand.
I forget the way those stones, that solid weight
against my knuckle, breaks
reflected light into sparks, cracks
a grocery store's ceiling glow
into such shards a young cashier,
says casually, as I bag
my broccoli, *I love
your ring.* And every time she does, I stop

for just a moment, trying to remember
what she means and then
what I should say—a plump and wrinkled woman
in jeans and a plaid shirt, a woman
who did not wash
her hair or smear on foundation

before she came to shop. In that split
moment, I calculate
a response appropriate for this girl as young
as I was that day I stood beside a bed
in a dark room stuttering something
polite to the heap of bedclothes, the old
aunt who lay with hands glittering
on the sheets and waited for her nurse
to dole out the next allotted
glass of gin. I stop bagging, just
a second, to hear my own voice years later

on the phone, *Mom, I can't wear
that. It's a flashlight!* But here, now,
in the checkout lane, I catch
myself and answer quick, *Oh, thanks.*
and add, as if an afterthought, *It's a family
ring*, before I go on filling bags
with rice and beans and milk
the way an old woman who wears diamonds should.

Saving the Garden
for Marnie

The vinca died again,
in that single spot near the front.
First one turned gray
in spite of extra watering.
It took days to go.

> Then two more shriveled, quickly
> *(There's nothing you can do)*

leaving only three green mounds
to unfold gold blooms along the border.
Everything else thrives—the rampant coreopsis,
the red and white impatiens spreading
almost perceptibly each night.
Even the salvia, this year, have survived
morning's forays by slugs.

> But there is a space, the plan of my English
> country garden interrupted.

Every year, the same:
nature intruding on my rule of order, stopping
the flow of hybrid colors.

I've learned to buy potted blooms
to fill an unplanned hole. This year
they are yellow, like small daisies.
(leaves so rough they might have grown on a roadside)

They look sturdy enough
to hold their own.

Looking For Jeffers' House

the night-herons by the flooded river
cried fear at its rising
Before it was quite unsheathed from reality.
                                    Hurt Hawks

Nothing was what I expected, not
the tiny cottage crushed on every side
among suburban stucco houses, not the stone
tower. It was short,
stolid independence almost
eclipsed by shingled rooftops everywhere.
Even the Pacific glimmered faint
between an angled maze of walls,
too quiet and too far away
to match the scene in my imagination.
Naturally, there were no hawks.

We had threaded a mire
of velvet golf courses, walled and landscaped
millionaire estates looking for
a painting by El Greco.
What we found was Norman Rockwell.
We parked the car, wandered
up and down the sidewalk empty-handed
until a dog's wild barking
drove us away.

The next morning as fog lifted
from an untamed rocky point,
I looked across the bay for where
we'd been. Surely it was no trick of sight
when the tower rose
among the houses as he
said it would, and
a shadow, dark and blinding, skimmed the waves.

What Hummingbirds Do

She hangs over my window feeder just an instant,
dips her bill, hovers skittish
and afraid, the way we all distrust
what we do not know, streaks away
then back to sip again.
Here in the East we see only those
called Ruby Throats. The males have all
the color. The female at my window seems
more gray than green without a spot of scarlet.

Once in a Southwestern city park
before flying home
I watched more hummingbirds, and different
than I had ever seen, come and go
from a feeder, beating copper and emerald wings,
flashing throats orange, violet, fuchsia.
A woman beside me on the bench murmured
their names—Rufous, Calliope, Black chinned.
When she stood to walk with me,
looking for other birds, her brown hair hung
flat and dull onto her back.

We moved slowly, exchanging details,
as women do, of our families grown away
and what we do when men
are not beside us. Suddenly this woman I had known
for half an hour said straight, *He's having an affair.*
Her hands fluttered up and dropped.
He said he stopped, but I know
that's where he is today.
My feet timed themselves with hers
in woods so dry twigs crunched with every step.

She talked of years of keeping house
and moving town to town with his career.
She told about dinners carefully prepared
for businessmen he brought around
her polished table, and her small future
as an artist always shrinking
with her years. *Should I stay?* she asked.
I who had made choices of my own
for other reasons long ago had scant advice.

At home my hummer pauses now outside the glass
to look at me, then turns her back
and settles tiny feet along the feeder's rim
to sit while she drinks the offered nectar long and slow.

Early Daffodils
After Shuri Kido

They rise like the remembrance
of something forgotten; blinding rays, sun
emerging from clouds (while a glittering net of rain still falls).
There is an electric jolt, like love
(the summer of our lives) returning
after a long-frozen winter of silence,
after spring's first warm breath, the thundering
crack of ice breaking across the pond we had been skating on

(the solid no longer something to depend on)

and green shoots, buds emerging through dead leaves,
along the shore. A glow bursts from brown land.
Bright flags end the siege, call truce to a silent war
(no shots have been fired).
 Tell me how a heart should feel
when the drawbridge suddenly reaches out
of its own accord, the bolted gate opens to welcome
    the weaponless enemy
without battle (the town alive with music and dance).

Love, show me how to rush out into the world again,
how to pluck and gather so much joy.
Teach me how to fill my arms with gold.

We celebrate another January anniversary

This afternoon could rival spring the way
the sun still blazes gold on leafless trees
at four, so brilliant even on this winter day
we forget the icy silence of our recent weeks,
those frozen hours. We've shed our hats and coats,
stopped our job of splitting wood to sit
here side by side against a bare-limbed oak
and bask in warmth as lovely as our sheets
an hour ago. A short break, then we're back
to our labors once again, ready to cut and haul
logs to the woodshed where we'll build a stack
as high as we can reach against the wall.
The years have shown us the need to prepare
for cold and the work it takes to build a fire.

Potter's Shop

It's the practice, she says.
I caress a polished bowl
big as a table top, perfectly round and even,
emerald expanse lush
with gigantic flowers.
My husband taps its rim
lightly, the touch you save for crystal.
Feel he commands. My fingers
vibrate on the far circumference.

She frowns. *People ask how long
it took to make this. I say "two weeks.
And 25 year*s." Those years it took
to raise our son. My husband
lifts his hand, turns to stare
at mugs, bowls, vases, plates—
rows of bare clay drying,
surfaces prepared for heat,
finished colors set in fire and gleaming
for those prepared to pay
and take them home.

*Some people say I charge too much.
Will they be wearing the same shoes in twenty years
when my mug still holds their coffee?*
I wander to the shelf of seconds,
flawed and brilliant.
My husband's gaze meets mine.
We have bought this weekend in the mountains
to learn each other's thoughts again.
We stray toward the door.

Come back when you are shopping,
she says and turns to make
a pot of tea, start her wheel.
On the outside path through her tangled patch
of daisies, mint, impatiens,
our hands touch. Ripe
blueberries spill across a split rail fence.

Taking Stock

There—a tiny you in your best Sunday dress
standing before Mama's bright orange beds
of unrestrained nasturtiums and marigolds tilting
in a breeze that made tall pines whisper overhead.

Sun-split days at Grandma's, her pink and yellow
roses tended gently until buds spread
into circling layers of velvet petals to be clipped
and artfully arranged in vases beside her rose-silk couch.

The first soil of your own, perched on a country hillside
behind a tiny house, rows lush with green beans
and tomatoes, squash and strawberries, ears of corn
tasseling to sweetness in their strong tight husks.

Later, flowering hedges around a bigger house outside a city,
beds of daffodils and crocus, shady edges green with hellebores,
and hostas, Solomon's seal. And at the center a sunny spot
of basil, cucumbers, and tomatoes golden as ripe plums.

Until a cottage surrounded by tall penstemons and daisies,
lilac bellflowers, white lilies, purple salvia, ruby roses,
a pear tree's branches drooping with the weight of ripening
fruit, and a row of raspberry clusters glowing in the sun.

And you, bringing in bouquets of red and yellow dahlias
with buckets of pears to peel and slice and boil, calculating how many jars
it's possible to load with jam and pickles, and asking how much more
you can still gather up before the last warm days of summer end.

In the Moonlight

The roof of the tent is almost stained-glass,
a diffusion of shadows, ghosts
of pines beyond the netted window

standing their black watch
against the western crescent's
silvery spread and stars'

bright net above. Silence,
punctuated by a soft lap of lake
on rocks and a flat plunk—

something slapping water. Close.
Then, far off, wails, calls
like the voices of lost lovers, roll

across the surface of everything. You
could believe it a dream conjured
in the half-light of your city apartment

to be tossed away into the dawn
were it not for the hum of tiny wings
beating against the screen beside your face,

or the small sting on your neck.
A buzz, while off in the dark another slap
resounds as beaver go about pushing

logs to the stream. A breeze
brushes soft branches
into a rush of whispers,

and the loons' distant moans and yodels
echo on, as you know they will,
long after you return home.

Louise Cary Barden writes poems that use sensory images of the natural world to share the private inner life we all lead. With a mother who read her poetry before she could talk and encouraged a love of literature, Barden first published a poem in a children's magazine at age three. During their childhood beside a small pond in Massachusetts, Barden and her closest sister Betsy grew up writing stories and plays (presented to parents by the neighborhood children), as well as a family newsletter.

Once she reached Hendrix College in her mother's home state of Arkansas, however, Barden saw herself as a reader more than a writer. Through her final year for a B.A. at University of Arkansas and then her study for a M.A. in English at University of Maine (where she followed her husband), she didn't take a single creative writing class. It was only after she spent eight years as a college instructor, became a copywriter and marketing executive with a major banking corporation, and joined an advertising agency that she began writing and sharing her poems, and studying the craft.

Along the way, life gave Barden lots to write about. When her husband became a National Park Service Ranger, they lived at Grand Canyon, The Grand Tetons and Acadia National Park. When he returned to graduate school after their son was born, they lived in a shot-gun house in the country outside Knoxville, Tennessee. Over the years she studied watercolor painting and photography, and amassed memories of the rich tiny details of the natural world around her. Later, Barden and her husband regularly visited the Canadian Quetico canoe wilderness, north of Minnesota. Those experiences helped her see and love the unspoiled environment she shares in her poems.

As a result, Louise Barden's work employs details drawn from nature to symbolize the internal joys, sorrows, fears and hopes of a long life, while she expresses her hopes of preserving the wild undamaged places she has experienced for the generations who will come after her.

This collection was a semi-finalist in the 2023 New Women's Vision competition. Barden has also won the Lois Cranston Prize (*Calyx* Journal), Oregon Poetry Association Members Choice award, the Harperprints chapbook competition, and others. Her poems have appeared in anthologies and journals including *Greensboro, Chattahoochee, Willawaw* and *Timberline Review,* and *humana obscura* and *Cathexis Northwest.*